REPEAT the SOUNDING Joy!

Christmas Medleys
for Piano Solo

Arranged by Melody Bober

Moderately Easy

PUBLISHING COMPANY

lillenas.com

Contents

Angel Medley   22
Includes: Angels We Have Heard on High *with* Hark! the Herald Angels Sing *and* Angels, from the Realms of Glory

Coventry Carol *with* **Carol of the Bells**   10

Ding Dong! Merrily on High *with* **He Is Born, the Divine Christ Child**   7

God Rest You Merry, Gentlemen *with* **Sing We Now of Christmas**   33

I Saw Three Ships *with* **Good Christian Men, Rejoice**   26

Joy to the World *with* **O Come, All Ye Faithful**   4

Manger Medley   30
Includes: There's a Song in the Air *with* Away in a Manger

O Come, Little Children *with* **O Little Town of Bethlehem**   36

Rise Up, Shepherd, and Follow *with* **Go, Tell It on the Mountain**   14

Still, Still, Still *with* **Silent Night! Holy Night!**   39

The First Noel *with* **It Came upon the Midnight Clear**   18

We Three Kings *with* **What Child Is This?**   42

Joy to the World

with

O Come, All Ye Faithful

GEORGE FREDERICK HANDEL
Arr. by Melody Bober

*"O Come, All Ye Faithful"

Ding, Dong! Merrily on High

with

He Is Born, the Divine Christ Child

French Carol
Arr. by Melody Bober

*"He Is Born, the Divine Christ Child"

Coventry Carol

with
Carol of the Bells

Traditional English Carol
Arr. by Melody Bober

Rise Up, Shepherd, and Follow

with

Go, Tell It on the Mountain

Traditional Spirituals
Arr. by Melody Bober

16

*"Go, Tell It on the Mountain"

The First Noel

with

It Came upon the Midnight Clear

W. Sandys' *Christmas Carols*
Arr. by Melody Bober

*"It Came upon the Midnight Clear"

Angel Medley

includes

Angels We Have Heard on High
Hark! the Herald Angels Sing
Angels, from the Realms of Glory

Arr. by Melody Bober

*"Angels We Have Heard on High"

*"Hark! the Herald Angels Sing"

*"Angels, from the Realms of Glory"

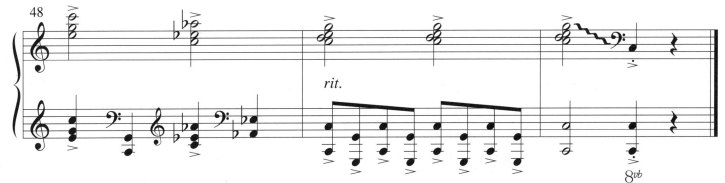

I Saw Three Ships

with
Good Christian Men, Rejoice

English Carol
Arr. by Melody Bober

*"Good Christian Men, Rejoice"

Manger Medley

includes
There's a Song in the Air
Away in a Manger

Arr. by Melody Bober

*Music by KARL P. HARRINGTON. Arr. © 2009 by Lillenas Publishing Company (SESAC). All rights reserved. Administered by The Copyright Company, PO Box 128139, Nashville, TN 37212-8139.

*"Away in a Manger"

*Music by JAMES R. MURRAY. Arr. © 2009 by Lillenas Publishing Company (SESAC) All rights reserved. Administered by The Copyright Company, PO Box 128139, Nashville, TN 37212-8139.

God Rest You Merry, Gentlemen

with

Sing We Now of Christmas

English Melody
Arr. by Melody Bober

34

*"Sing We Now of Christmas"

O Come, Little Children

with
O Little Town of Bethlehem

Traditional
Arr. by Melody Bober

*"O Little Town of Bethlehem"

Still, Still, Still

with
Silent Night! Holy Night!

Austrian Melody
Arr. by Melody Bober

40

Tempo I ♩ = ca. 72

We Three Kings

with

What Child Is This?

JOHN H. HOPKINS. Jr.
Arr. by Melody Bober

*"What Child Is This?"

REPEAT the SOUNDING *Joy!*

Angel Medley
Includes: Angels We Have Heard on High *with* Hark! the Herald Angels Sing
and Angels, from the Realms of Glory

Coventry Carol *with* Carol of the Bells

Ding Dong! Merrily on High *with* He Is Born, the Divine Christ Child

God Rest You Merry, Gentlemen *with* Sing We Now of Christmas

I Saw Three Ships *with* Good Christian Men, Rejoice

Joy to the World *with* O Come, All Ye Faithful

Manger Medley
Includes: There's a Song in the Air *with* Away in a Manger

O Come, Little Children *with* O Little Town of Bethlehem

Rise Up, Shepherd, and Follow *with* Go, Tell It on the Mountain

Still, Still, Still *with* Silent Night! Holy Night!

The First Noel *with* It Came upon the Midnight Clear

We Three Kings *with* What Child Is This?

lillenas
PUBLISHING COMPANY

DISTRIBUTED BY HAL LEONARD CORPORATION

ISBN 978-0-8341-7702-4

71901327 $14.99